All God's Children Gotta Sing!

Easy Anthems for Two-part Choirs

Lloyd Larson · Mary McDonald · Ruth Elaine Schram
Larry Shackley · Jean Anne Shafferman · Natalie Sleeth

MW00710861

Contents

Also available:

Accompaniment CD (99/3333L)

Editor: Lloyd Larson
Cover Design: Kati Hufford
Music Engraving: Linda Taylor

ISBN: 978-1-4291-3971-7

A Lorenz Company • www.lorenz.com

Fount of Every Blessing

Two-part Mixed with opt. Trumpet*

Words by
Robert Robinson, 1758,
and **Lloyd Larson**

Arranged with New Music by **Lloyd Larson**
Based on NETTLETON,
Traditional American Melody from
John Wyeth's *Repository of Sacred Music*

⏺ indicates CD track number.

*Trumpet part is available as a free download. Visit www.lorenz.com and search for 45/1178L.

*Ebenezer: "Stone of help" (I Samuel 7:12)

to Jerome and Anita Gathers

Lord, I Know I Been Changed

Two-part Mixed

Traditional Spiritual Arranged by
Larry Shackley

JD

you don't be-lieve___ that I have been___ re-deemed,___ The

just an-gels in heav-en done signed my name.___ The

fol-low me down___ to that ol' Jor-dan stream.___ The

14

45/1178L-14

Sing a New Song to the Lord

Two-part Mixed

Arranged by
Jean Anne Shafferman

Words and Music by **Natalie Sleeth**
Incorporating *TALLIS CANON*

www.lorenz.com
LT

*Tune: **TALLIS CANON**, by **Thomas Tallis**, ca. 1561.

23

45/1178L-23

That Promised Land

Walk Together, Children/When the Saints Go Marching In

Two-part Any Combination

Arranged by
Ruth Elaine Schram
Traditional Spirituals

Walk to - geth - er, chil - dren, don't you get wea - ry. There's a

great camp - meet - in' in that prom-ised land. Oh,

(opt. Part I)

(opt. Part II)

walk to - geth - er, chil - dren, don't you get wea - ry.

(I)   (II)

Walk to - geth - er, chil - dren, don't you get wea - ry.

Walk to-geth-er, chil - dren, don't you get wea - ry. There's a want to be in that num - ber,_____ when the

great camp - meet-in' in that prom-ised land. Oh, saints go march - in', march - in' in. Oh, when the

great camp - meet-in' in that prom-ised land. There's a saints go march - in', march - in' in. Oh, when the

My Shepherd Will Supply My Need

Two-part Mixed with opt. Flute*

Based on **Psalm 23**
Isaac Watts, *alt.*

Arranged by **Lloyd Larson**
Tune: RESIGNATION
from *Southern Harmony,* 1835

*Flute part is available as a free download. Visit www.lorenz.com and search 45/1178L.

I walk___ through the shades of___ death Your___ pres - ence is my stay;_____ one___ word of___ Your sup - port - ing___ breath drives___

To my children, Beth and Chris

Stand Up!

Two-part Mixed

Words by
George Duffield, Jr., 1858

Music by
Mary McDonald
Incorporating **WEBB**
by **George J. Webb**, 1837

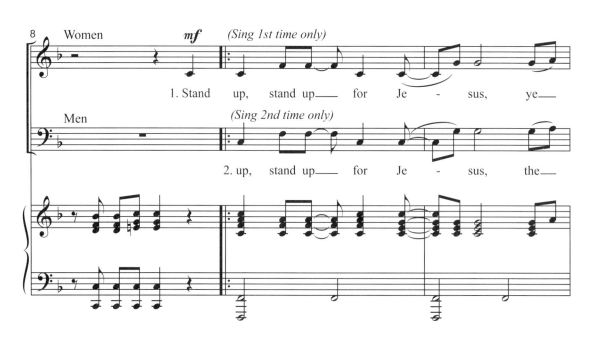

Good and Simple Gifts

Unison or Two-part Any Combination*

Arranged by
Jean Anne Shafferman

Words and Music by **Natalie Sleeth**
Quoting **Simple Gifts** and Old Hundredth

*For performance by unison voices, sing Part I throughout.

 JD

54

45/1178L-54

gifts com-eth from the Lord, com-eth from the Lord, our God. Praise Him

gifts com-eth from the Lord, com-eth from the Lord, our God. Praise Him

ev - 'ry - day.

ev - 'ry - day.

O praise the Lord!____

O praise the Lord!____

Go Ye Therefore

Two-part Mixed

Words by
Mary McDonald
based on **Matthew 28:19-20**

Music by
Mary McDonald

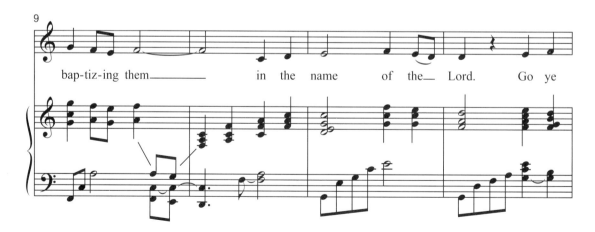

www.lorenz.com JD

And lo, I am with you al-ways, I am with you e-ven un-til the end of the world. Go in my Name, I am

And lo, I am with you al-ways,